It'll Be ok, Lucy

By Starla Criser   Illustrated by Sharon Revell

Thanks, Angie.

-S.C.

No part of this publication may be reproduced, stored in a retrieval system, or transmitted in any form or by any means, electronic, mechanical, photocopying, recording or otherwise, without permission of the publisher.

For information regarding permission, write to Starla Enterprises, Inc.,

Attention: Permissions Department,
9415 E. Harry St., Ste. 603, Wichita, KS 67207

ISBN: 978-0-692-94596-4

Text copyright @2017 by Starla Criser
Illustrations copyright @2017 by Sharon Revell

All rights reserved. Published by Starla Enterprises, Inc.

Printed in the U.S.A

"Lucy! Lucy!
Bella raced into the bedroom.

"It's time to go!"

Go? Where?
Lucy looked up from nibbling on a cherry.

To the beach?

"We're moving today. Remember?"

Bella picked up her backpack from the bare mattress.

"To North Carolina. It's a long way from here."

Not to the beach?
Not to run on the sand?

Lucy really liked to do that.

She didn't understand.
What is moving?

Was that why boxes were stacked in their room?

The boxes made her nervous.

"It's so exciting! A new home. A new bedroom."
Bella smiled in happiness.

"A new stepsister, almost my age. And a new step-dad."

"Oh, Lucy, it's so very exciting!"

Lucy's tummy felt funny, she was worried.

New people? What if they don't like me?

She would miss their pretty pink bedroom.

She looked out the window at the beach.

She would miss playing there with Bella.

Worried, Lucy started to roll into a ball. She always felt safer that way.

Bella put down her backpack. She walked beside Lucy's cage.

She reached down to gently touch Lucy.
"I promise it'll be okay."

When Bella stepped back, Lucy picked up her cherry. She held it close to her.

Her heart raced.

I don't like change.

But I trust Bella.

"I love you, Lucy,"
Bella said with a smile.

Lucy tried to smile back.

I love you, too.

Bella picked up her backpack again. She put it on her shoulders.

Lucy spotted her wheel. She raced over to jump inside it.

Running always made her feel better.

**Run!
Run fast!**

Bella's mother, Madison Torres, walked into the room, smiling at Lucy.

"You don't need to be worried."

Lucy scrambled out of her wheel.

I can't help being worried.

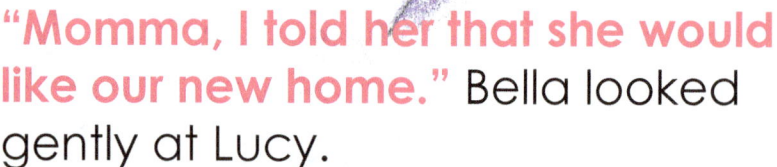

"Momma, I told her that she would like our new home." Bella looked gently at Lucy.

Lucy looked at the boxes in the room. They still made her tummy feel funny.

I like this home. Why do we have to move?

"Change can be good, Lucy," Madison said. "You'll like Bella's new stepfather, Ethan Sanders. He's a very nice man."

Madison smiled at her daughter. "Bella likes him, right?"

Bella nodded. "Oh, yes, Momma! I like Cassie, too."

She leaned closer to Lucy. "Cassie is my new stepsister."

But what if they don't like me?

"The moving truck is almost loaded," Madison said.

Bella danced around in excitement. "It's about time to go, Lucy!"

Lucy squeaked softly and hurried into her bed.

I'm safe now!

Lucy stayed in her bed as Madison carried her cage to the van. She was so nervous.

She liked riding in the van with Madison and Bella. She liked going places.

But she would miss their house on their beach.

They drove through tall mountains. Bella excitedly told Lucy all about them.

Bella helped Lucy to see a tall arch in St. Louis, Missouri.

And Lucy saw a big, muddy river in Memphis, Tennessee.

On and on they drove. Lucy spent a lot of time running on her wheel.

If she ran fast enough, they would get there soon.

Run fast! Run super fast!

On the third day of driving, Madison said, **"We're here!"**

Bella leaned toward her window. **"The house is so big, Momma!"**

Is that good?

Lucy had liked their small house on the beach.

Lucy froze, nibbling on a pea pod.

Maybe I should run again in my wheel.

Bella gently lifted Lucy from her cage. She held her close to her chest.

"I'm so excited. Aren't you, Lucy?"

I'm not sure.

Lucy saw Bella's smile fade away. She looked a little worried.

That made her worried, too.

What's wrong?

Lucy heard a noise beside the car window.

A girl with blonde hair and a smile said, **"We've been waiting for you."**

Bella smiled back and lowered the window.
"Hi, Cassie!"

Lucy looked at the other girl, feeling a little unsure.

The girls were kind of alike...but different.

Lucy was different, too. She was small.

And she had lots of spines.

"**This is my hedgehog, Lucy,**" Bella said.

Cassie smiled at her. "*She's so cute.*"

Lucy wiggled her nose in greeting. She was curious now, not worried.

Something moved inside Cassie's pocket. Lucy heard a quiet squeak.

What is that?

Smiling, Cassie pulled a small animal with crazy red hair from her pocket. **"This is my guinea pig, Sophia."**

Sophia squeaked again and smiled at Lucy. She wiggled her nose, just like Lucy sometimes did.

Lucy squealed back in excitement. She liked Sophia already.

Sophia squeaked again and they all looked at her. She wiggled, trying to get down.

Lucy squealed and squirmed, too. The girls giggled.

A tall man walked up and stopped next to Madison and the girls. He put an arm around her shoulder.

"Cassie and I are glad you're here," he said.

His smile was warm as he looked at Bella, then at Lucy.

Lucy snuffled her approval. She liked the kindness in his eyes.

The girls took Lucy and Sophia to Cassie's room. They would all share it for now. It had green walls.

"Dad and I are still painting your new room. It will be pink," Cassie said.

Pink! Yes, yes, yes! Bella and I like pink.

Lucy squeaked to Sophia.

Lucy liked this room...for now.

The girls carefully set Lucy and Sophia down in Sophia's cage. Lucy looked around curiously.

The toys were like hers, even the yellow ball and the pink wheel.

Sophia climbed onto her bed and looked at Lucy.

Then Sophia smiled at Lucy.

I'm happy to share my toys with a new friend.

A new friend.
A bigger family.

Lucy's heart felt good. She did a little dance of joy.

It was all okay...just like Bella and Madison had said it would be.

Character List

Lucy   **Sophia**   **Bella Torres**

Cassie Sanders   **Madison Torres**   **Ethan Sanders**

Other Books By Starla Criser

Blossom and Matilda Series
Blossom is an adventurous and curious cow with a vivid imagination that she shares with her friends on the farm.

Book 1 - **A Family for Blossom**
Book 2 - **Blossom Sings With Her Friends**

www.ingramcontent.com/pod-product-compliance
Lightning Source LLC
Chambersburg PA
CBHW082248300426
44110CB00039B/2484